Humanity in the Machine

What Comes After Greed?

Humanity in the Machine

What Comes After Greed?

By Brian David Johnson

YORK HOUSE PRESS

ISBN: 978-0985550868

York House Press
1266 E. Main Street, Suite 700R
Stamford, CT 06902

YorkHousePress.com

Cover design by Sandy Winkelman
Book design by Lisa Lawlor

CONTENTS

INTRODUCTION TO THE SERIES HUMANITY IN THE MACHINE

Werner Heisenberg was a German theoretical physicist who was one of the core founders of quantum physics. Early in the twentieth century, quantum physics upended the science of the world as we knew it. For centuries Newtonian physics defined how scientists saw the universe. Set out by the English pioneer Sir Isaac Newton, these classical mechanics explained the motion of objects in space. But in 1905 everything changed.

Albert Einstein, along with Heisenberg and a small band of pioneers, began to explore the invisible world. This was the universe at the Plank scale, it was sub-atomic, and it acted in spooky ways. Einstein actually said the action of these sub-atomic particles had "spooky action at a distance." Things are just weird in quantum physics. Teleportation is possible and distance actually breaks down.

Later in Heisenberg's life, after he had won the Nobel Prize, he wrote a series of books and gave lectures exploring the implications of the new science that he had helped create. During the winter of 1955 to 1956, he gave a series of lectures at the University of St. Andrews. The last lecture was called "The Role of Modern Physics in the Development of Human Thinking." In it he points out that "in the history of human thinking the most fruitful developments frequently take place at the points where two different lines of thought meet."

Heisenberg understood that it is the intersection and sometimes collision of ideas that create the best results. From the violence of their impact can spring new perspective, fresh ideas, and possibly new insights.

This collision of ideas is the force behind the series you are now reading: Humans and machines. Often they are thought of as sitting at opposite ends of each other; many draw a thick, dark line between the two. On one side you have us humans, and on the other side you can find all of the machines and technology of our times.

But what happens when we take these two different lines of thought and bring them together? Can we gain new insights about our world, ourselves, and the technological future we are rapidly approaching? Let's see...

***

What is a machine?

A machine does the work of people. A machine is a device or system that is used to assist in a human task. That machine can be a physical or mechanical device like a wheel, lever, axe, or any other of our early machines. A machine can also be an electronic system like a computer, network, or software that assists with a human task. The actual form of the machine doesn't matter that much. What does matter is what the machine does—it aids us humans to accomplish a task that we would normally do on our own. It amplifies and extends our abilities.

A machine is also a tool. A tool by itself is just a tool, a physical or electronic item used to accomplish a goal. A hammer is just a hammer. Human beings love to get enamored by our tools. We fixate on them. We love our technology and gadgets. But a tool is still just a tool and becomes meaningful only when we explore how that tool can be used. What piece of human work will it do? How will this machine ingeniously extend our capabilities? A hammer is just a hammer and is really meaningful only when we realize it can build a house. What makes a machine truly useful is when we can use it to touch the lives of people and make their lives better.

What is humanity?

There is nothing simple about this question. It has been a debate, a discussion, and an argument that has been raging as long as there have been humans to ponder it. Very simply, humanity is the condition or the quality of being human. Humanity is that part of us that defines us as individuals and as a society. It is that sometimes elusive thing that makes us who we are.

What is Humanity in the Machine?

Machines are built by humans. We imbue our machines with our humanity. When we design and build technology, we include our culture, our sense of ethics, and even our expectations for the future in our constructions. Our machines become extensions of ourselves. Tools are designed to do the work that humans would do, so there is a part of that machine that must also comprehend who we are as people. Our technology is an extension of our humanity. We build our humanity into our machines.

But what part of ourselves will we build into our machines? Are we conscious of the decisions we are making when we build the complex systems that surround us? As we move into the future, there will only be more technology and machines in our lives. People find the pace of technological advancement to be staggering and hard to comprehend. But have we asked: What do we want from all those machines? How will they fit into our lives? How will that change our world?

***

The Humanity in the Machine series explores the interplay between who we are as a human society and the machines and technology we are building. We investigate the tension between our values and unbounded possibilities of breakthrough innovations. We navigate the often tricky balance between the past we treasure and the society we are becoming. Ultimately we embrace the fact that the future is built every day by the actions of people. Every one of us builds our own future. But we must first ask ourselves: What kind of future do we want? What kind of future do we want to avoid?

It is in these explorations of our humanity and our machines that we can understand the possibilities that lie before us and the perils that we wish to avoid.

***

Sir James Hopwood Jeans was an English physicist, astronomer, and mathematician. Like Heisenberg, the phy-sicist we met earlier, Jeans distinguished himself with a career exploring quantum physics, but he also made great contributions to the theory of radiation and stellar evolution. In one of Jeans' last books Physics and Philosophy (1942), he explores the implications quantum discoveries on the rest of our lives. He wanted the book get people to think differently about the world around them. Like Heisenberg, he was taking very different lines of thought and bringing them together. He asked, "Is the world we perceive the world of ultimate reality, or is it only a curtain veiling a deeper reality?"

James closes the book with this: "It can hardly be a matter for surprise that our race has not succeeded in solving any large part of its most difficult problems in the first millionth part of its existence. Perhaps life would be a duller affair if it had, for to many it is not knowledge but the quest for knowledge that gives the greater interest to thought—to travel hopefully is better than to arrive."

This "Humanity in the Machine" series explores both today's and tomorrow's difficult problems, pulling from surprisingly different lines of thought to peruse an alternative perspective, giving us a new and varied vision for our future. These collisions of ideas may not give us clear answers, but it is the asking of the questions that is most important. We must always remain curious and strive to understand both our humanity and our machines.

ACKNOWLEDGEMENTS

First and foremost I must thank Penelope Holt who proclaimed me to be her "soulful futurist" and was the driver behind this entire project. I'm indebted and in awe of the people who helped, educated and lectured me about this subject; their passion and generosity was amazing and this project could have never happened without them. Thank you to the writers, journalists, historians and economists whose work helped to inform and illuminate. Thanks to Robert Black for his help. Finally, a note of exceptional gratitude to my favorite economist – Paul Thomas. I hope he never tires of my strange questions. 25.

Part One

GETTING TO GREED

It's kind of weird to be writing a book about greed. I'm a technological futurist. It's my job to develop a vision for what it will feel like to be a human and live 10 to 20 years from now. I'm an atypical futurist, because I refuse to make predictions. I feel it's my responsibility to develop visions for a future that we can then go and build. Using a mix of social science, technical research, economic forecasts, trend data, global interviews, and even a little science fiction, I develop these actionable models for corporations, trade organizations, and militaries.

I'm also an optimist. As a futurist, declaring myself an optimist was one of the most radical things I've ever done. It seems that most people like their futurists to be pessimistic, spewing doom and gloom. But I can't do that. I believe that the future is made every day by the actions of people. If this is true, then why wouldn't we build an awesome future? Let's not build a future that sucks.

Now why would a technological futurist want to explore greed and what comes after it? Good question. It really all started about three years ago…

The Day It Happened

It happened at 2:45 pm on May 6, 2010, and lasted just two minutes. Like most people, I didn't really hear about it until the next day, when I saw headlines that said things like, "Computers Crash the Stock Market," "Glitch Sends Stocks Plunging," and "Panic Sends Dow into Record Dive." This was the Flash Crash of 2010, and it gave me chills.

When I heard that the computers had crashed the stock market, my stomach knotted up. This was bad. It wasn't the Dow Jones loss and recovery of about 1,000 points that worried me. It was the effect it would have. I had been doing research looking out to the year 2020 and thinking about data. I called it "The Secret Life of Data." The idea was that as we enter the age of Big Data, those data will begin to take on a life of their own. Our data will begin to do things for us. We'll have machines talking to machines and computers talking to computers, and we humans won't always know what's going on. Being an optimist, I could see all the amazing things this could do for us. It could make people healthier, more productive, and even more sustainable.

But on May 6, we saw the dark side of the secret life of data, and it wasn't good. *ABC News* reported that no one had any idea how *the Flash Crash* had happened and it scared the hell out of everyone.

But what had caused the machines to crash the stock market? I had vaguely heard about a thing called algorithmic trading or high-frequency trading but didn't know much about it.

I've always been fascinated with how computers have transformed our financial systems, from online banking to the global markets. One of the more exciting and scary places that have completely altered how people make money is algorithmic trading (I later found out people just call it "algo trading") and a subset called high-frequency trading (known as HFT). Both of these use computers and algorithms to make stock trades and make money at a pace almost as fast as the speed of light.

Algo trading is both cool and scary. It's cool because any business that has the speed of light as an essential component for doing business is pretty badass. It's scary because of the shroud of mystery it wraps around itself. And it's even scarier when demons pop out of the dark cloak in the form of the flash crash that affects real people where they are most vulnerable: their wallets and their retirement funds. It seemed the algorithms were messing around with our future.

Technology radically transformed the twentieth century. This shouldn't surprise anyone. Machine and technological advancements have transformed the lives of humans for about as long as we've had technology and humans. And there's no indication that this will change anytime soon.

The twenty-first century looks like it's going to be a doozy. Computers, computational intelligence, and data are primed to have a good couple of decades, altering how we humans live, work, play, and love. By 2020, it is estimated that there will be more than 20 billion computers being used by just 9 billion people. That's more computers than there are people on the planet. In 2013, the computational power of most smartphones is greater than the entire amount of computer horsepower that the United States used to get to the moon and back. As I write this, the social networking company Facebook is valued at more than $80 billion—and this is a business that doesn't actually produce any physical goods. The company essentially makes computer code, 1's and 0's. I don't think this is a bad thing, but I do think it shows how much our lives have been transformed by machines and computational intelligence.

The single clear goal of algo trading is profit, to make money and make a lot of it really fast. If these machines have so much control over our lives and our money, how do we imagine what the future might be like? How do we decide what kind of future we want? I wanted to understand it enough so I could chart out the different future we wanted to avoid. That's what got me to greed.

To imagine what our future might be like, I started

exploring one of the nastier sides of who we are as humans: greed. Greed isn't pretty. It ranks pretty high on the Christian religion's list of seven deadly sins that will get you an express ticket to hell. On the list, in the Book of Proverbs, 6:16–19, greed is number three.

In most definitions of the word, you'll find the first example is almost always linked to money: *selfish desire for money* or *an excessive desire for money.* Money, it seems, is cozied up close to greed. That nasty little cocktail of greed and money gave me a case study to explore on the secret life of data and some tough decisions we need to make in the coming years.

To model how it will feel like to live in the future and ask the question what comes after greed? I went futurehunting. For over a decade I've been exploring what it will feel like to live in the future. Once I've done this, I hit the road and look for instances of that future happening today. People used to joke that I was going around the world "futurehunting." Hunting down the future. The joke stuck.

I went futurehunting the future of greed, but more importantly, I wanted to find out what comes next. If using computers to make and lose money on the stock market is our present, then what's our future? If we're using all of this computational intelligence to maximize profit and make money now, then what comes next? What if we ask ourselves: What comes after greed?

Part Two

UNDERSTANDING THE MACHINES

As we start futurehunting, we need to have an understanding of the underlying technology that is enabling algo trading. Let's demystify the technology and science so we can clarify what we're looking for. Our first step is to understand the machines.

There are three things you should know about the technology:

Lesson One: Algorithms Are Simple

The technological systems that enable algo trading are a mix of high-speed data networks, powerful computers, and the software that runs on them. The data networks and computer systems are no different than the ones you have in your home or office except that they are much faster. The software, however, is very different. At the foundation of this software is something called an algorithm, and it gave algo trading its name.

Algorithms might sound complicated and mystical, but they aren't. Algorithms are quite simple. An algorithm is a series of steps that a computer programmer tells a computer to take that will give us an output. An algorithm or code is the language computers use to talk to each other. It's a language like any language; it's how we talk to the computers and how the computers talk to us. If you think how many computers we have in our lives today and the fact that we are only going to have more in the future, you can see that understanding computer programming and algorithms is as important as knowing English, Spanish, Mandarin, or any other language on earth.

But at the heart of code and algorithms are a series of simple steps that get us to an outcome. One of the earliest kinds of algorithm was a simple recipe. Like an algorithm, a recipe is a series of ingredients, portions, and steps that need to be followed in a specific sequence to produce the dish.

Let's use a recipe from one of my favorite chefs as an example. Bill Granger is an Australian chef who has created a series of successful restaurants and cookbooks. Bill is known for his simple food that's never fussy and always delicious. One super-easy and amazing recipe (algorithm) is the one for Bill's chocolate cake.

Ingredients:
250g unsalted butter, softened
440g sugar
4 eggs
250 ml milk
310g plain flour
5 tsps baking powder
1 tsp vanilla extract
4 tbsps cocoa powder

Steps:
Beat the butter, sugar, eggs, milk, flour, baking powder, vanilla, and cocoa powder with electric beaters for about 8–10 mins until the mixture is pale and well combined. Pour into tin and bake (in 350-degree oven) for 40–45 mins or until a skewer poked in the middle comes out clean.

The directions for making a chocolate cake could look like this:

Butter + sugar + eggs + milk + flour + baking powder + vanilla + cocoa powder
Then
combine for 8–10 mins
Then
40–45 mins in 350-degree oven
= Chocolate Cake

A recipe is a series of steps that you take in a sequence that gives you a desired output: the dry stuff plus the wet stuff, combine for 8–10 minutes, then bake in a 350-degree oven for 40–45 minutes; this gets you a chocolate cake.

The algorithms that are used on Wall Street are like Bill's chocolate cake algorithm, just more complicated. Over the past two decades, the dramatically increasing power of computers has allowed a new generation of software programmers to author extremely complex recipes that scour various information feeds for the ingredients for their cakes. In the case of trading on Wall Street and around the world, the ingredients are the now-massive amounts of data available from the trading markets themselves as well as the global Internet. The desired output of this recipe is just as sweet as chocolate cake and even more desired: profit.

There's more than one kind of algorithm that can be used for stock trading. In her 2013 *High Frequency Trading* textbook (Wiley), Professor and quantitative trader (this is the industry jargon for a person who uses computers, data and algorithms to trade stocks) Irene Aldridge details four distinct kinds of trading that can be performed using computers and code (listed slowest to fastest):

1. Systematic trading: "computer-driven trading decisions that may be held a month or a day or a minute and therefore may or may not be high frequency" (speed: purposely slow)

2. Electronic trading: "the ability to transmit the (trading) orders electronically as opposed to telephone,

mail or in person" (speed: efficiently fast)

3. High-frequency trading: "known as HFT, this uses algorithms and the extreme speed of computers to make stock transactions faster than any human ever could" (speed: approaching the speed of light)

4. Algorithmic trading: known as algo trading, "a variety of algorithms spanning order-execution processes as well as high-frequency portfolio allocation decisions" (speed: all of the above and constrained by the speed of light)

Generally, the blame for the Flash Crash of 2010 is placed on HFT and algo trading. The rapid-fire buying and selling in the case of the 2010 crash was mostly selling and dumping shares that caused the uncontrollable loss. What frightened everyone so much on that day wasn't just that the algos were crashing the market, but the speed with which they could do it.

Lesson Two: Algorithms Are Written by People

Much like Bill's recipe for chocolate cake, all algorithms are written by people. I often tell people that all code is a kind of science fiction story. We are writing these algorithms with a future end in mind. Like all great chefs (and Bill is self-taught), we cook in our heads and have a specific output in mind. That vision of the future might be a delicious chocolate cake, or it might be algo trader's huge single-day profits. That's one of the things to remember about algo trading and HFT: unlike most investors in the stock market, that HFT trader ends the day without any holdings. The trader isn't investing in the market. The trader is making money from the market. It's all about maximizing profit. (We get to this later.) They start the day with no stocks and end the day with none as well.

Algorithms are written by people, and that means that they have a point of view. Our technology is imbued with the hopes, values, and world view of the people who created it. In this sense, the algorithm is simply an extension of the person who wrote it. The only difference is that once complete, the trader's creation can execute on that vision with greater speed than any human being.

By design, algorithms are limited in what they can look for. In trading circles, they call these signals. A person creating an algorithm must decide what signals or feeds of information the person is going to tell the algorithm to keep an eye on. At this time, it's impossible for any algorithm to watch everything; we don't have the complexity or the computational power to pull that off. So for the moment, we need to tell our algorithms to look in some areas for information and ignore others. This is one way the programmers transfer their world view into the machines.

The problems arise when we realize that our high-speed algorithm is now only living in a very constrained world. It doesn't live in the real world. It lives in a world that is bounded by the constraints we have given it.

A great explanation of this is our humble chocolate cake. In the world of a chocolate cake algorithm, life is simple. We look for the wet ingredients (butter, sugar, eggs, and milk), then we look for the dry ingredients (flour, baking powder, and cocoa powder), and finally we look for an oven and hang out for a half hour.

The problem with this is that Bill's recipe is all well and good in a world where there are only chocolate cakes. But we know the world is much more complicated and wonderful than that. Who wants to live in a world where we only have chocolate cakes? To our chocolate cake algorithm/recipe, there is no other reality. There are no strawberry cakes in the world. We have made the decision to limit what our algorithm can see. Worse than this, in the world of the technology we have created, there is no such thing as strawberries. Literally strawberries don't exist. The limits can be dangerous.

Lesson Three: Machines Are Stupid

For all their power, algorithms and the computers and networks they run on can only do what they are told to do. Bill's cake algorithm can't turn around on its own and start playing chess. The power behind the algorithms is also their weakness. They can only do what people program them to do. These machines are programmed to do specific tasks in a very specific way. If they don't get the data they need, or if they need to deviate from their programmed path, they simply don't work, or sometimes they even crash.

For his 2010 book *The Speed Traders*, Edgar Perez, host of the High Frequency Trading Happy Hour in New York, had a conversation with Richard Flom, vice president of trading for Systematic Alpha Management. Among the many topics they discussed was how HFT should be managed. Flom said, "I think we could all agree that if we locked up an algorithm and let it trade on its own for 10 minutes, we would find that a lot of things will go wrong."

Most of the algo traders in Perez's book agree that people cannot be pulled out of the equation. Most of these traders use the algorithms as just another tool in the rather large bag of tricks to make money from the markets.

There have been examples when the algorithms have been allowed to trade on their own with disastrous consequences. Probably the most popular example is the "Knightmare" on August 1, 2012. For 45 minutes, Knight Capital Group lost more than $450 million when one of its high-speed trading algorithms was left "locked up" too long. It nearly destroyed the company.

These algorithms are incredibly powerful, but they are also incredibly limited by design.

Part Three

I GO INTO THE BLACK BOX

As a futurist, a big part of my job is having a clear and actionable understanding of the future. But the other part of what I do is to travel the world talking to people about that future and looking for examples of how that future could be happening today. The science fiction writer William Gibson wrote, "The future is already here — it's just not very evenly distributed." This part of my work is futurehunting: searching for examples of the future happening today so that we can understand the human, cultural, social, and other impacts it could have.

Because of futurehunting, I was fascinated with HFT and algorithmic trading. As we enter the age of Big Data and a time when we are living in a world surrounded by increasingly more intelligent computers, the sometimes murky and frantic world of HFT seems like a perfect futurehunting example of the future we are moving toward. HFT is an instance of the future playing itself out today. The Flash Crash of 2010 was the dark side of it.

Now that we have an understanding for how the technology works, let's dig into the world of algo trading. What makes it tick? What do the practitioners have to say about it, and what are its broader implications?

When people talk about this world of financial machines, they often refer to something called the "black box." This is a term used in high tech to describe a system that is a complete mystery. No one knows how it works except the people who designed it, and they won't tell you about it. Black boxes worry people because the person who built and uses the black box has all t he power.

This mystery is especially dangerous when the black box starts to malfunction, like it did during the Flash Crash of 2010, and people get hurt.

The Rise and Stall of Algorithmic Trading

"I want to talk to you about algorithmic trading," I said into the phone. "I'm interested in high-frequency trading because it's a kind of secret life of data."

"The peak of all this algo trading has happened," Alan Wexelblat said quickly and with an easy assurance. "It's over."

Alan is a designer. Starting in 2008 at Lime Broker-age, he designed interfaces for the software for high-frequency trading. He not only had a front-row seat to the rise of algorithmic trading, he was in the game. Lime Brokerage is a sophisticated technological brokerage firm known for its high-performance, low-latency infrastruc-ture (meaning they have really fast data connections) and market-neutral best execution delivery (meaning they are unbiased as to the markets they choose to trade and do business in). They don't trade their own funds. For this reason they were touted as neutral because they don't do in-house trading. Lime won the "Biggest Innovators on Wall St" award from Security Technology Monitor and "Most Cutting-Edge IT Initiative" award from Ameri-can Financial Technology.

Alan is a good guy. He's married with two boys that are 13 and 10. Like most dads, he's worried his sons are growing up too fast. Alan talks with the speed of an automatic weapon, and most of the time when he's talking about algos, he's deadly serious.

"The first time I was really introduced to the world of algos and high-frequency trading was when I came to Lime in 2008 and was talking with Tony (Anthony Amicangioli) the CTO at the time. He used a white board to outline his vision for 'Brokerage 2.0.' His idea was to make an equities brokerage built from the ground up around the idea of HFT. He wanted automation to replace nearly everything that floor traders traditionally did. That was the fall of 2008."

"What did you think when you understood what he was talking about?" I asked. "What did it feel like to hear about HFT for the first time?"

"To me the big idea, the real thing, never was HFT itself. I thought the really big idea was always about what you could do if you assumed that HFT was just table stakes...what if that was just the beginning."

The Flash Crash of 2010 may have brought algorithms and high-frequency trading to the public's attention, but it had caught the eye of a few reporters a little earlier. On Friday, July 24, 2009, nearly a year after Alan had seen it for the first time, high-frequency trading hit the media mainstream.

Charles Duhigg wrote a piece for the *New York Times* that described nothing good with the technology of the practices of HFT. Duhigg wrote, "Powerful computers housed right next to the machines that drive marketplaces like the New York Stock Exchange enable high-frequency traders to transmit millions of orders at lightning speed and, their detractors contend, reap billions at everyone else's expense. These systems are so fast they can outsmart or outrun other investors, humans and computers alike. After growing in the shadows for years, they are generating lots of talk."

On August 9, 2010, just three months after the flash crash, the New York Stock Exchange (NYSE) opened its Mahwah, New Jersey, data center.

"While the change won't be noticeable to stock traders or investors, it's a significant moment for the growing market for low-latency trading," wrote Rich Miller for *Data Center Knowledge*. He continued, "The new data center features colocation space for trading firms seeking high-speed access to the matching engines. NYSE Euronext says it has sold out all the available colocation space in its first phase at Mahwah—reported to be at least two 20,000 square foot pods."

Staff reporter for the *Wall Street Journal* Scott Patterson explained the effect of Mahwah on the world of trading in his 2012 book *Dark Pools*, writing, "The (New York Stock) exchange was all but dead. Mahwah was the new floor, a powerful confluence of capitalism and state-of-the art computer technology. While tourists snapped photos of the exchange's marble façade on the corner of Wall and Broad, the real trading was taking place thirty miles away in Mahwah's vast air-conditioned floors of computer servers."

Why did trading firms need to be co-located with the new hub of the NYSE? Because in the world of algo trading, the speed of light matters. There are few businesses in which the speed of light really matters, but in the world of high-frequency trading, pushing up against the speed of light is an integral part of the entire industry. The thing that allows the algos to make so many trades so quickly is that they are hooked directly into the massive servers that now run the world's trading markets. Like the NYSE's Mahwah data center, trading no longer takes place as it had for most of the last two centuries. Gone are the days of frantic traders yelling "Buy!" and "Sell!" on the floor. Today, all trading happens via computer code in a server. It all happens in a black box.

Like the NYSE, most markets give some trading firms direct fiber optic access into the trading servers. In a fiber optic cable, data (the old "Buy" and "Sell" yells of the traders) travel via light. Light can only go so fast (also known as the speed of light). When you want to make a trade faster than your competitor, where you put your server matters, because the speed of light matters.

Let's pretend you and I are competing to buy a stock on the NYSE at the cheapest price. You and I both send our "Buy" order at the same time. Whoever buys the stock first get it at a lower price than the person who comes in second, because you and I are buying so much stock that the value of the stock will go up when either of us buys it. Your server is based in Chicago, and my server is cozied up next to the NYSE servers in New Jersey. When we hit "Buy" at the same time, I win, because both of our "Buy" commands travel at the speed of light but my "Buy" command has less distance to cross, so I get there first. I win. You lose. When you're dealing with the speed of light (also known as latency), distance matters.

Technically what I've just told you is wrong, but it's wrong at a micro level. Rarely does one order sweep out the liquidity - that's one reason bids and asks are often in lots of 100. What happens is that I get it for a penny less than you do. This is assuming we're talking generic highly liquid stocks. A hundred pennies means I paid a buck more on that trade. That doesn't seem like a lot, but if I'm trying to move 100,000 shares that's a thousand trades and I'm "losing" a buck on each which means it cost me a thousand dollars more to move my shares than I anticipated.

When it's HFT versus HFT that extra buck eats up a lot of their profit margins. These days margins are a few pennies on a trade, so losing a whole dollar on a single trade means a lot. For an institutional trader dealing in volume a buck doesn't mean anything. But consistently losing those bucks drives your costs way up and institutional houses move quantities in the millions or tens of millions of shares. At those volumes the pennies really add up. (Alex helped me with this detail.)

For the last few years, most trading markets all over the world have gone digital and made money by giving the HFT trader mainline access to the markets. It meant that everyone had to get into HFT and algo trading just to remain competitive. It became known as the arms race, and everyone had to escalate their speed and computational power. Everyone had to design better algorithms and even algos that watch what the other algos are doing. It kept going like that, up and up and up. More speed. More flash crashes.

In April 2013, the Associated Press's Twitter feed

was hacked, and it reported that the White House had been attacked and President Barack Obama had been hurt. As a result, the algorithms watching these signals, assuming an attack on a White House would lead to a drop in the stock market, instantly started dumping their shares. "The S&P 500 lost $121 billion of its value within minutes," *CNN Money* reported, "but quickly rebounded."

Just recently, reports have come out that these highly publicized flash crashes are not the only crashes that are happening. There are "mini flash crashes" each day, creating wild fluctuation in single stocks. On April 22, 2013, the value of Google's stock plummeted, only to shoot back up again.

When I was talking with Alan about this he noted, "The Google incident is unusual. I've read the recent reportage and I think it's sensationalist crap. It's signal fluctuation that corrects itself so fast humans can't even perceive it except by poring over detailed logs long after the fact. People who are stupid design algos with hair triggers and get caught by these twitches. My sympathy for people with badly design algos is very small."

This kind of behavior is prompting people to think that the algo traders are engaging in stock manipulation. Not a new practice for the world markets, but they are using new, high-speed tools to do it. (We'll come back to this in just a moment.) But Alan also thinks this is "sensationalist crap." "If it's deliberate, and I tend to follow the maxim that you should never assign to malice that which can be adequately explained by stupidity, then it's likely a ploy used by some bots to try and sniff out other bots that are shadowing them," he explained. "It's the digital equivalent of a well-executed head-fake in basketball."

The arms race continued to escalate into 2013. There were more HFT companies, and most of the large trading companies had HFT departments. Some people made a lot of money; many people lost. That was until it all stalled out.

On June 6, 2013, Matthew Philips reported in *Bloomberg Businessweek* that "for the first time since its inception, high frequency trading, the bogey machine of the markets, is in retreat."

New York's Rosenblatt Securities estimated that HFT traders are making fewer trades; 2012 saw 1.6 billion trades, down from 3.25 billion in 2009. Worse than that for the traders, they are making less money. The HFT industry made $1 billion in 2012, down from the $5 billion in 2009.

"It's like the Internet bubble back in the 1990s," Alan explained to me. "You had a lot of interest and a lot of money. Anyone with a business plan suddenly became an entrepreneur and people were giving them millions of dollars. But that didn't mean they were good at running and growing a business," he said, and laughed. "It just meant that people gave them money and when the money ran out most of them collapsed and went away. It's the same with algo trading from 2008 to today."

Alan was right. "The profits have collapsed," Mark Gorton of Tower Research Capital told Philips for his *Bloomberg* article. "The easy money is gone." Philips goes on to note that "a number of high frequency shops have shut down in the past year."

"We're going to be left with two kinds of people using algo trading," Alan said as he wrapped it up for me. "You're going to have the big institutional investors and the dogs. The institutional investors are the guys who are buying stocks and holding onto them like traditional firms. They are in it for the long haul. They use the algos just to get the best price when they are buying and selling."

"And the dogs?" I asked.

"The dogs are the ones who know what they are doing. They are the ones who are really good at this. They are so good that they are doing what they are doing and we probably won't know about it."

"Wow," I said; I couldn't stop myself.

"Yeah," Alan continued. "They are the mathematicians and the physicists that are really good at getting their algos to make money. The life span of one of these algos has dropped dramatically. When I started it was six months. If you came up with a good algo you could keep it running and keep it making money for about six months. That was in 2008. Today the life span is about six weeks if you're lucky. That's what the dogs are good at. They change how things are done. They are really good at optimizing for profit."

It's Always Been about Profit, Stupid

It was a cold and overcast day in Sydney, Australia. I had come to the Southern Hemisphere to collaborate with a colleague of mine. Dr. Genevieve Bell is one of the world's leading cultural anthropologists with a specialty in how technology impacts the lives of people.

"I'm looking into algorithmic trading," I said as we walked through the streets of central Sydney.

"Of course you are," she said as she smiled at me over her glasses.

"It's on the decline and it's a great case study for how people will act and interact with data in the future," I continued. "The data literally has a life of its own—sometimes it makes people rich and sometimes it crashes the stock market."

"So what do you think about it?" she asked.

It was still early in the city, and most of the shops were closed up tight. Genevieve and I had just finished breakfast outside the Sydney Museum and were walking over to the Museum of Contemporary Art Australia. In a few hours, we were going to give a two-hour talk on some joint research we've been doing together. Over the past few years, we've been exploring how our collective imaginations and visions for the future push us to develop radically different technologies.

"I don't have an opinion on it yet," I explained. "The entire algorithmic trading industry, all over the world, is designing its technology for one purpose only—profit."

"That makes sense," she replied, looking into the window of a store.

"But I'm wondering if we can optimize for something different," I went on. "That might sound kind of odd, but I think we might be able to imbue our technology with something other than profit, and the algo trading world is doing it today. If profit is all about greed, then what comes after greed?"

Genevieve was quiet for a time. This was a good thing. I've worked with her for more than a decade, and I know when she's got something in the steel trap that is her brain. She was thinking, and that was good.

"Go look at the stock market," Genevieve said as the always-boisterous Australian birds squawked overhead. "Has it always been about profit and greed?" she asked. "I think it probably has, but how did they define profit back when they set up the New York Stock Exchange? Not only that, how did they set up the Chicago exchange or even the London exchange? That goes back centuries. If you can figure out what they value and what they are striving for, then you might be able to figure out how to change it."

"So I need to track down a historian," I said.

"Yeah," she continued. "How has it changed? Is algorithmic trading something different altogether from what the exchanges were set up for originally?"

We turned down a street, and it started to feel like it might rain. I looked in through the front windows of a gallery that hadn't opened yet. "Originally it was about raising capital, raising money to build a business," I answered.

"Are you sure?" she pushed.

"I'll go find a historian," I replied.

A Conversation with a Deceased Historian

I really wish I had gotten to meet Robert Sobel. Sadly, the historian and 43-year Hofstra University professor passed away in 1999 at the age of 68. Sobel was a nerd for the stock market. I say this with utmost respect. His book *The Big Board*, written in 1965, was the first history of the NYSE written in more than a generation. Sobel was a master of the history of financial markets and the people who made and broke them. I've spent a lot of time with Professor Sobel writing this piece.

When you read Sobel's extraordinarily detailed historical accounts of the stock market or U.S. financial panics, you learn (like Genevieve thought I would) that it's always been about profit, stupid. Not only that, it's always been volatile and messy. The history of markets of the U.S., and even the history of the world markets, is a long chain of panics, crashes, optimism, prosperity, and then panics and crashes (rewind and repeat).

For most of the history of humans, business has been all about the sole proprietor: that person with a great idea or just the get-up-and-go to put together a business that solves a problem for people and makes money doing it. It was not until the seventeenth and eighteenth centuries that things got more complicated. (I'm about to overgeneralize here, so please, all historians and Professor Sobel, excuse me.)

"The rapid expansion in trade, the increase in the amount of money in circulation, and the enlarged vision of the merchant-capitalists led to the speculative orgies of the seventeenth and eighteenth centuries," Sobel writes in the beginning of *The Big Board*. These large expeditions, like opening up trade with South America, required a tremendous amount of capital. To raise the money, companies were set up and shares were offered in the endeavors. This was the beginning of our modern stock trading system.

One of the best examples of the orgies of this time came in London in 1711 with the South Sea Company. "In 1711, several businessmen and nobles received a charter for the South Sea Company, which was granted a monopoly of trade with South America. The venture prospered...[and became] the most powerful instrument of the state," Sobel explains. The number of shares of the company went from 130 to 300 and then even further up to 1,000. "This success led investors to look into other companies for similar profits."

Many of these new companies were legitimate, but many were sheer frauds out to bilk money from investors. "Firms were proposed to manufacture perpetual motion machines, provide better funerals for mendicants [I didn't know what this was. They are also known as beggars, but a specific kind of beggar that is more religious. Not a bum, more a religious person who doesn't work and depends on people to live], cure sick horses and transmute animals [I had no idea what *transmute* meant. *Merriam-Webster's Collegiate Dictionary* defines *transmute* as "to change or alter in form, appearance, or nature and especially to a higher form." So I'm guessing *transmute* means somehow cutting up animals and taking them to a higher form. Wow. Who wouldn't invest in that?]. One apparently successful company, in terms of the rise in its stock price, was to manufacture radish oil, which had no known use. Another, which oversubscribed, was 'A company for Carrying on an Undertaking of Great Advantage, but Nobody to Know what it is.'" The bubble burst within the year.

As you walk with Sobel through history, you begin to see quite clearly that these booms and busts and panics are not out of the ordinary. On the contrary, they are the norm. They are so normal, in fact, that you can chart the history of the U.S. financial market by looking at its crashes and panics. Sobel's 1968 book *Panic on Wall Street* does just that.

In the beginning of his book, Sobel cites John Stuart Mill, an English philosopher, political economist, and civil servant. Mill was seen as one of the most influential philosophers of the nineteenth century. Mill wrote, "Panics do not destroy capital; they merely reveal the extent to which it has been previously destroyed by its betrayal into hopelessly unproductive works" (*Credit Cycles and the Origins of Commercial Panics*, 1867).

Sobel goes on to point out, "Financial panics have been endemic to America, as to all western countries." I found this bit the most illuminating. The idea that crashes and panics are native to the U.S. financial system is hard to take, but the evidence is there. "Most panics were made possible, though not necessarily caused, by weaknesses in the financial structure. American banking was notoriously slipshod and inadequate after the disestablishment of the second Bank of the United States [This was a private corporation under charter to the American Government from 1817 to 1836. It was liquidated in 1841] and before the formation of the federal reserve...Faulty banking practices appear as important contributing factors in (the panics) of 1836, 1857, 1873, 1893, 1907 and 1929."

Sobel ends the book about panics by saying, "What this means, in essence, is that we may undergo another 1962 [This is considered to be the first flash crash. The market crashed so quickly and the volume of shares being sold was so high that the stock ticker couldn't keep up. It took the little device more than an hour after the market had closed to report all of the market activity], and in some circumstances, we could have a far more severe crash. Since the economy is more complex today than it was in 1929, it would be more disastrous. It is to be hoped that such an eventuality will not come to pass, but the possibility should be faced that a thirteenth chapter (Sobel's book had 12 chapters) the most unfortunate of all—in a book of this nature may well prove necessary." Hello 2008!

As you read through Sobel's exhaustive histories, you see pattern after pattern. The history of the financial markets, more specifically the history of U.S. financial markets, is a tale of speculation and booms and busts and manipulation.

Come on, you can't hear a historian from the 1960s talking about faulty bank practices and complex markets leading to a panic and crash that did happen in 2008 and not see the pattern.

The game of Wall Street, the game of the financial markets, and in fact the game of all finance is optimizing for profit. The only desired outcome is profit, and the entire game is optimized for that. Whether we're talking about the South Sea Company, a company founded to cut up animals and bring them to a higher state, or a financial bubble inflated by risky mortgage-backed securities, it's all about doing whatever needs to be done to lower risk and increase profit. These are the rules of the game.

A Quick Chat with a NYSE Journalist about History both Distant and Recent

We did an early release of this book for the TEDx-WallStreet event, held at the end of October 2013 in New York City at the New York Stock Exchange. As a part of the event I gave a talk on "What Comes After Greed". I have to tell you that standing in the NYSE and talking about how we might be able to optimize for something other than profit and greed was a strange and exhilarating experience. I half expected them to carry me off the stage and throw me out of the building. But they didn't. Everyone seemed to embrace the idea and wanted to talk more.

At the event I met Bob Pisani. If you are a follower of Wall Street and financial news you know Bob really well. He's a financial commentator for CNBC and has been a journalist covering the NYSE from the floor for over a decade.

I asked him about his take on HFT and where he placed it in the history of Wall Street.

"HFT is simply the latest technological manifestation of the most fundamental drive in the stock market: to get actionable information before anyone else," he explained. "Once you see the entire history of the stock market as nothing more than a bunch of investors who are trying to one-up each other in the information department, then HFT is neither mysterious nor amazing."

The reason they weren't amazing to Bob was because of his experience as a journalist. He could see their technology and its place in the long history of financial markets.

"I've often said that Nathan Rothschild was the first high frequency trader," he told me. "Rothschild had agents stationed at the Battle of Waterloo in 1815 and received news that Wellington had defeated Napoleon nearly 48 hours before anyone else in London. Rothschild began buying up government bonds, reasoning that interest rates would soon drop. He kept buying, and did not sell until late 1817, when bond prices were up more than 40 percent. Niall Ferguson estimates his profits were 600 million pounds in today's money.

"Rothschild and his brothers had already made a fortune smuggling gold to Wellington's troops on behalf of the British government. They were paid handsome commissions because no one had the physical or intellectual network to move so much coin. The massive amount of movement of gold caused pricing inefficiencies, which he exploited. He had a banking network, which consisted of his brothers in London, Frankfurt, Amsterdam, and Paris. It was so fast and efficient; they could take advantage of the price arbitrage. If gold was higher in Amsterdam than in Paris, they would sell gold in Amsterdam for bills of exchange then send them to Paris, where they would be used to buy gold."

It became clear to me that it was all about the rules of the game and how people could take best advantage of technology and systems to win at the current financial game.

"There are similar stories for the railroad, the telegraph, the stock ticker machine, the Quotron machine, and the traders on the floor of the NYSE," Bob finished up. "I guess you could say I've been assembling a history of technology disruption in the stock market. Maybe I'll publish it someday..."

That's a book I'd love to see!

I explained that my journey started with the Flash Crash of 2010 as an example of what could happen when our technology begins to act on its own. He had been there, on the floor of NYSE and I was fascinated to hear what it was like.

"You need to be careful on why the Flash Crash happened," Bob cautioned. "It's a real minefield. It's the intersection of market structure, global economics, and politics. Just be careful here."

"What's your take on it?" I asked.

"Back in 2010 markets had already been under pressure by concerns of a European meltdown, specifically over a debt crisis in Greece. Early that afternoon at least one mutual fund firm executed a series of very large sell orders in the stock futures market that, because of the way the orders were structured...They are structured to be a certain percentage of the market volume, so when the volume increased, the amount of selling increased proportionally... because of this they became an exacerbating factor in the decline.

"Also, some exchanges reported receiving pricing irregularities from the other exchanges...You have to bear in mind that this happens in sub-second intervals..."

"It's nearly the speed of light," I added.

"As a result, some exchanges declared "self-help" against the other exchanges." Bob continued. "This is a way for each exchange to declare 'I'm not sure I understand your data.'

"When market participants, particularly HFTs, saw this, many of them...but not all of them...shut down their trading. They did this because they cannot trade when the have bad quotes, bad bids and offers. It was this drying up of liquidity was also a major exacerbating factor in the decline."

From Bob's view on the floor of the NYSE the Flash Crash of 2010 was a confluence of events and conditions. It wasn't just one thing; not a single algorithm, not a single trader but a chain of events that fed into one another until things went really wrong. But it was interesting that so much of went wrong on that day had to do with data. The algorithms and the markets thought they were getting bad data so they shut down. The rules of the markets and the motivations of the algorithms fell one after the other, leading to a swift and terrifying crash. To understand the rules of the financial game better, I went to a guy who had spent his life studying the global finance: An economist.

A Conversation with a Living Economist

Paul Thomas is the chief economist at Intel Corporation. I've collaborated with Paul for years and have a great relationship with him. He comes out of the airline industry and is widely respected. I think he's awesome, and he thinks I ask interesting questions that economists would never ask.

"It's not all about profit," Paul explained to me. "If you want to understand the markets and the rules of the game, as you say, then you have to understand that it's not all about profit. "Well, it's not just about profit in markets. Profit is not the god of financial markets, but it's a good intermediary. But sometimes it can lead us away from what we really want to do."

"Profit is not the god of financial markets," I repeated. "But it's a good intermediary." I chuckled as I wrote it down. "Paul, you are one of the most quotable economists I know."

"I'm not sure profit is the problem in what you're looking at," Paul continued. "As I understand it, you're worried that if we are optimizing all these algorithms and high-frequency trading for just profit, then it will lead to problems."

"That's part of it," I replied.

"I don't think it's just profit," Paul explained. "We have several mechanisms to keep people and markets in check. We have laws that say, yes, go and maximize profit, but do it this way and don't do it that way. If you do it that way, say, like insider trading, then you go to jail. So profit is just the first step."

"True, we could create specific laws around what the algorithms do," I added. "The SEC is always looking into things like that."

"We also have social structures that keep us in check. And also, if I understand your way of thinking, if we keep ourselves in check, then we will keep our algorithmic creations in check." Paul paused. "Often companies are ostracized and sometimes even shamed into changing their profit practices. So it's not as simple as profit alone."

"What if we wanted to optimize for something other than profit?" I asked.

"Brian, it gives economists nothing but great consternation to consider optimizing for anything other than profit," Paul replied.

I burst out laughing, writing frantically. "Paul, you really are the funniest and most quotable economist I know!"

I don't think he was amused.

"I think, you could optimize for something other than profit but I also know that profit maximization is an attractor," he continued. "What I mean by that is that the strong link between ownership and control will tend to lead to concentration of resources in the hands of those people who do maximize profit."

"Ok.." I replied but wasn't following.

"Maybe that's too dense a way of expressing my point, so let me expand on it. If you control a business firm that sells goods or services, then your control probably follows either from your dominant ownership of the firm or the relationship you have with the owners. It could also come from your employment as the manager of their assets.

"Now suppose you have a big heart and devote a

good deal of your effort toward maximizing not profits alone but some combination of profits and social goals. Unless the social goals are coincident with profit maximization, then you would be leaving money on the table, as people say. This would attract takeover offers from other potential owners."

"Why's that?" I asked.

"Well your firm's market value would be evaluated in terms of the income stream that it generated," he explained. "That stream could be larger if the firm were to be run in a fashion closer to profit maximization. Just the promise of higher profits from moving the firm closer to profit maximization would allow new investors to take over the firm as an leverged buy out.

"Even if you were a single owner dedicated to more than profit maximization and you turned down the offer, even this would not be a safe guard. If your industry is fairly competitive, then the profit-maximizing segment of the industry could underprice the goods and services produced by the competing social value-maximizing firm and drive it you company to extinction. In other words, if you don't run your firm as profit-maximizing enterprise, the firm is unlikely to survive."

"Does that mean the economics of buisess require that everything must be optimized for profit?" I asked.

"No nesesarrily," he answered. "There are sustainable firms that have bragging rights on social responsibility. There are even successful mutual funds that concentrate their holdings in equity of socially responsible firms."

"But what about the profit maximization…" I started.

"I suspect that socially responsible firms are exactly those firms that have managed to combine profit maximization and socially responsible behavior," Paul said quickly. "Let's look at one of the best known socially responsible investment funds, namely Calvert Equity Portfolio. (By the way their symbol is CSIEX.)

"Calvert's website for the fund states that, 'the Fund seeks to invest in companies and other enterprises that demonstrate positive environmental, social and governance performance as they address corporate responsibility and sustainability challenges.' Morningstar reports that the top 10 holdings in the fund are CVS Caremark, Apple, Google, Qualcomm, Microsoft, Danaher, Coca Cola, Cameron, Costco, and Gilead Sciences. Of these firms, only one is in an industry with a poor social image, namely Cameron, which manufactures and markets energy extraction equipment.

"Many of the other firms are in industries that are consistently viewed as socially responsible in part because profit maximization in these industries requires environmentally clean operations and encourages good employee relations. So, for example, it is hard to see how Microsoft's or Google's operations could be more profitable if they were dirtier. Costco could choose to emulate Wal-Mart's lower employee pay but that would presumably result in the same inefficient high employee turnover that hurts Wal-Mart.   In fact, there may be halo effects from belonging to industries with good images that protect these companies from more critical appraisals."

"Ultimately is it about a kind of synergy?" I asked. "We need to find a synegy between profit maximization and the values of the company. The two combined have a greater effect."

"Yes," Paul replied. "The values and motives have to be clear. We may not be able to get away from profit so we really have to think long and hard about what else we're adding to the mix. It could mean great success or assured failure."

Part Four

WHAT ARE YOU OPTIMIZING FOR?

The futurehunting had been successful. I had a pretty good understanding of the reality of algo trading, how it played out in the financial markets, and how it affected people. As I had hoped, it gave us a great case study for how the secret life of data could become real. There were the good, the bad, and the ugly. We saw examples of dark, foreboding possibilities for disaster, but also the boring reality that algo trading was just a tool that had become common and was even falling out of favor.

But more importantly, we could use this beyond just Wall Street. If we build technology and technology is an extension of our own values and dreams for the future, could we actively change how we develop that technology? Could we optimize it for something else?

What Does a Futurist Eat for Lunch?

Pulling the food containers from my lunch bag, I snapped them open with a crisp "pop" and set them on the conference table. Lama Nachman, a colleague and fellow principal engineer, watched me with a perplexed look on her face. I was used to this.

I'm kind of a funny eater. For the past ten years, I've pretty much eaten the same things every day. Where my wife sees every meal as an opportunity, I on the other hand eat like a small woodland creature. Picture a lot of fruit, vegetables, nuts, dairy, and protein. Because of this, I bring my lunch to work when I'm in the office. Again, picture a lot of little easy-snap plastic food carriers. One for nuts. One for baby carrots. One for cottage cheese. Also there's an apple, but it doesn't need a carrier.

As I happily munched away like a squirrel or chipmunk, Lama watched. I'm quite fond of Lama. She's an amazing engineer (if you own a smart phone in the future, there's a good chance you'll be using a piece of her technology). She's also a passionate and opinionated lover of wine (she likes cabernet; I like Barbera, and never the twain shall meet), and she has tremendous laugh. At that moment I was getting the cold, critical eye of the engineer. She was staring at my food.

"Yes?" I snapped a baby carrot in my teeth.

She said nothing.

"Would you like a carrot?" I offered her one. She didn't

reply. "They're good for you," I added.

"What are you optimizing for?" she asked, finally looking up at me for a moment, then back to the neat little containers.

"What?"

"What are you optimizing for?" She pointed at the food. "I can see you are optimizing for something with the combination of foods, but I can't figure out exactly what you are optimizing for. Is it vitamins? Calories? Is it…"

I explained the nutritional balance of fruit, vegetables, protein, dairy, fiber, and the rest.

"Ah," she nodded, pleased with my explanation. Her face relaxed, and she sat back in her chair. "That makes sense. 'Cause I could see it was something, but I couldn't figure out what you're optimizing for."

"I eat like an engineer," I said, taking a bite of apple. "It's like an equation or algorithm to me."

She laughed. "Well, I'm an engineer, and I don't eat like that." She took a bite of her pizza.

"No, you are an engineer," I fired back. "But you eat like a teenager."

She laughed so hard she nearly shot a piece of pepperoni at me.

As I was researching HFT and algo trading, my mind continually came back to this quick little lunchtime chat deep in the heart of Intel. Aside from its being a pretty good example of geeks talking at lunch, it also perfectly describes how an engineer thinks.

What Are You Optimizing For?

In engineering, this is one of the most important questions. What are your requirements? What is the outcome you are looking for? If you can identify this, you can then go and make it so. This is at the very base of engineering, making or creating anything.

In 2012, engineer and scientist David Blockley defined engineering in his succinct book *Engineering: A Very Short Introduction* (Oxford Press) like this: "Engineering is the discipline of using scientific and technical knowledge to imagine, design, create, make, operate, maintain and dismantle complex devices, machines, structures, systems and processes that support human endeavor." The British Parliament brought together a committee to define the essence of engineering and came up with an even shorter conclusion: engineering was "turning ideas into reality." To bring an idea into reality, you first have to have the idea. You have to have a vision and an opinion.

As we have seen, our tools and technologies are built by people. We imbue our tools, like the HFT algorithms or a hammer or anything else, with our own sense of humanity. Just look at how many different varieties of hammers there are. Blockley calls this out in his book: "Many people still regard the products of engineering as morally and ethically neutral—in other words, they are intrinsically neither bad nor good. What is important, according to this view, is how we humans use them. But engineering is value-laden and socially active—our tools have evolved with us and are totally embedded in their historical, social and cultural context. Our way of life and the objects we use go hand in hand—they are interdependent parts of our culture."

If our engineered machines and technology are an extension of us and filled with our values, then it is even more important to ask Lama's question, "What are you optimizing for?"

How Is the Stock Market Like a NASCAR Race?

It had been a long, hot August day in Bristol, Tennessee. I had spent the day with my wife and our good friend Kevin, wandering around the RVs and pre-race extravaganza that is Bristol International Motor Speedway. I was at a NASCAR race.

Have you ever been to a NASCAR race? It's awesome. The sound of 43 cars roaring past you is hard to describe. It's not that it has to be *heard*, it's more that it has to be *felt*. That much metal moving in a tight pack is a mass of physical force. If you want to learn about optimization, you have to go to a NASCAR race. Bristol is a half-mile short track with incredibly high banking in the corners (you'd never guess when watching it on TV, but you can barely walk up the corners they're so steep) and a lot of beating and banging on the cars. Bristol has been rated as the loudest NASCAR track on the circuit, earning its nickname Thunder Valley.

It's really crazy loud. The entire oval track is surrounded by stadium seating that can cram in 165,000 screaming fans. The August race is a night race, so the entire place was lit up and blazing with excitement. The race started, and as I stood in front of my seat (I don't think anyone actually sits at Bristol) and looked down at the tightly packed field of 43 stock cars, that amazing sound roared past me. It's deep and thunderous, and you feel it in your bones more than you hear it. But at the same time, there's a high-pitched whine of machines and technology being pushed to their very limit—and it never stops. It goes round and round and blasts up at you each time the field of cars passes by. Standing there yelling my head off, I couldn't help but think that this is what CERN, the European Organization for Nuclear Research, must sound like.

You might think it's odd that I would compare the sound of a NASCAR race to the massive Large Hadron Particle Collider (LHC) in Switzerland, but I think it's true. The particle accelerator whips those particles around and around, faster and faster, then finally smashes them together so that the physicists at CERN can pick through the massive amounts of data in their now-successful search for the Higgs Boson and other mysteries of our world. The Higgs Boson is sometimes called the Higgs particle. It's an elementary particle whose existence was first theorized by Peter Higgs in 1964. The particle's existence was confirmed in 2013 at the LHC.

The detection of the Higgs Boson could lead to a whole new science of physics.

I know a few guys who work at CERN, and they'll tell you that being at the LHC is a physical feeling. It's the largest machine built by humans, and the speed, power, and collisions are tremendous. It's the same thing in NASCAR. These incredibly complicated machines are built by a team of mechanics and engineers who finely tune the car for each track, and then make precise adjustments throughout the race to continue tuning the car. A half-pound more of tire pressure in the right-side tires gives more grips. Putting a "round" into the spring shocks of the car stiffens how the car drives. A tiny piece of tape can give more down force on the car so that it handles better. There is nothing simple about NASCAR. My wife calls it math at 200 miles per hour.

You might be asking yourself what this has to do with the secret life of data and algo trading. Simple. It's all about what you're optimizing for.

***

"Hey, there. This is Michael Waltrip speaking," he said with a bright southern accent.

"Good morning, Michael, it's a pleasure to speak with you," I said quickly. I was a little nervous. It was a little hard for me to believe I was actually on the phone with Michael Waltrip.

Waltrip is a NASCAR driver, commentator, and

team owner. He's won the Daytona 500 (NASCAR's equivalent to the Super Bowl) twice, in 2001 and 2003. I've spent many Sundays watching NASCAR races and Waltrip. He's known for his knowledge of the sport and big sense of humor. Through a really generous friend, I was connected with Michael and Michael Waltrip racing.

I explained to Michael about the ideas behind *Humanity in the Machine* and that I was looking for examples to think differently about computers and financial systems. I wanted to talk to him because each week he and his team have to make specific decisions about what they are optimizing for. The tracks are different, the weather conditions are always changing, and little optimizations can mean a lot.

"A NASCAR race car is kind of like a computer program," I explained. "It's like an algorithm. It's a complex machine that you have to tune specifically for what you want it to do on the track. Then you literally start it up and see how it performs. It's a lot like the financial algorithms I've been studying."

"The crew can tune the motor to run and get better gas mileage or get optimal power," Michael explained. "The differences aren't great, but when you're trying to win a race, that tuning is a very important part of the whole weekend plan. So you're right: the car is programmed."

NASCAR is extraordinarily high tech. Before the race, the team's engineers tune the cars using a computer system, making precise settings for how the car will operate during the race. These races can last up to four hours or more. Once they make those decisions, they can't go back and make any changes. The changes are too deep in the car. They simply have to figure out what they are optimizing for, set up the car, and then let it run.

"It's programmed to do what we ask it to do," Michael continued. "Ultimately it's the driver who has to get everything out of the car that he can," Michael said, and he chuckled. Being a driver himself, he knows that it's not all just about the technology. "But we use computers to maximize what he can do with the car."

A NASCAR race car is a highly complex system. The engineers who program the car optimize for conditions based on their experience and the testing they have done.

"I should tell you Scott Miller, our executive VP of competition, just walked in," Michael said. "I thought he'd be interested in our conversation as well."

"That's great," I answered. "Scott, how do you think technology has affected the sport? Michael and I were just talking about how a NASCAR race car is like a computer program."

"As an industry, we're using a lot more data," Scott answered. "We've developed better tools to make use of that data. We use it to make specific decisions about the car and how to get it ready for each race. But the other piece of the equation that you don't hear people talking about is historical data. We gather a lot of information over time about the nuts and bolts and springs and shocks on the car and how they work at one particular race track versus another. Then there's the human factor, the driver's feet, the human experience. Those three pieces of data go into our cars; historical data, human experience, and the real time data are what ultimately gives us the information we need to make our decisions about the car."

"Is it all about optimization?" I asked. "Is there a specific part you find the team optimizes for each track? Do you make different decisions about how to position and angle of the spoiler on the back of the car? Is it different for each track?"

"Well"—Scott started with an odd sound in his voice—"that used to be something we did, but NASCAR pretty much mandates the height and width of the spoilers. They give a specific spoiler with a NASCAR part number on it and we use that."

"Oh, I'm sorry," I said, and laughed, realizing that the strange sound in Scott's voice was his way of being polite that I was so behind the times. "I guess that shows you how long I've been watching NASCAR. Sorry about that."

"It does have to come from NASCAR," Michael jumped in. "It has to go at a certain place and it has to have a certain angle. No option. But that's just another example of the optimization we need to do."

"How so?" I asked.

"First there's the rule," Michael explained. "But then we can ask ourselves how do we optimize the template of the body of the car so that we put more air under that spoiler. Or we can change the design of the body of the car to take air off the spoiler." Spoilers on race cars are used to harness the power of the air moving over the car. Depending on the track and the desired optimization, that air can lift the car up or force it down on the track. "So, while NASCAR puts a rule in place that says we have to use a specific spoiler, they also give us a race car body that we modify. It's not as simple as changing the spoiler angle like we used to, but we can still optimize for specific results."

I started to see a pattern that NASCAR drivers shared with algo traders, a hyper-focused ability to optimize and continue to optimize. If one feature or tool in their tool box gets taken away, they'll find another way to get their desired effect. These changes could be small or large, but all are designed to give their car and driver or their algorithm the ability to win. For NASCAR, it's about winning races. For algo traders, it's about profit.

What's the other thing that NASCAR has in common with the stock market? They both have crashes. Some of those crashes are small, like a mini flash crash. A single driver will have a problem. The engine might blow up; they might cut a tire and hit the wall. But other times, the crash can be huge and fast and there's nothing the drivers or the crew chiefs can do about it but watch. In NASCAR, they call it the "Big One" when multiple drivers get hung up in a horrific tangle and smash of metal and rubber.

"What's it like to be part of a big crash as a driver?" I asked Michael. "What kind of goes through your head? This is your job, but you have to deal with crashes every day."

"When you come up in a sport like this, you race against a lot of people you know," Michael replied. "In some cases, I've had friends who got killed racing cars. You know, wrecking is dangerous. You're going 200 miles an hour and you're strapped into a steel cage, dangerous, but racing is much safer than it used to be. To tell you the truth, I worry more about not giving my team a chance to win if I crash. Personally, I don't think about it. You think about winning. I know I'm going to get it, but I just think about driving hard. I don't think about the aftermath. I'm going to do my job, and whatever will be, will be."

NASCAR has done a fantastic job over the past decade of making the cars and tracks safer. It is a testament to the skill of the engineers that very few people get hurt and most drivers walk away from the grisly crashes with no injuries except for being angry and frustrated. The sport has safety gear all over the cars and track because the entire sport knows that crashes happen.

That's what I really saw in the stories that Sobel showed us throughout the history of financial markets. The history of the stock market and trading is a history of crashes and panics. It's also a history of people and the government trying to safeguard people and the markets from those crashes. Also like NASCAR, the engineers will always push their cars to the edge of the rules, trying to squeeze out the smallest advantage over the other drivers/traders.

I asked Scott and Michael about this.

"I think there are strong parallels between what you two do and the financial rules and regulations," I said. "I really do think that a NASCAR race is a lot like the stock market."

"The restrictions in NASCAR and in the stock market are a lot alike," Scott answered. "It's about optimizing every little parameter you can to give yourself an advantage. It's never one sole thing."

"You're optimizing for a lot of little things," I added. "Multiple things at once."

"When you say 'optimize,' I think it's our job is to optimize the rules," Scott replied after a moment. "We have to take advantage of all the rules so that we can be the best that we can be. So optimization is really about how you lead and how you take advantage of every piece of the car that you possibly can."

But how much regulation do we need, and why? How safe is safe? What are we optimizing for? When you always know there is going to be a crash, are you optimizing for speed or safety?

At the High Frequency Trading Leaders forum in 2010, HFT trader Ben Van Vliet said, "[With] NAS-

CAR [for] example, we all want to race fast but safe. It doesn't do any good if someone crashes into the innocent crowd and kills people. There are external people who may be affected when things crash. What we want the government to do is to create a safe track for us to race fast. And if they are going to put speed bumps in there the racers are going somewhere else. And we won't be the center of the financial world anymore. So somebody has to create the environment, because if the regulation is too heavy-handed and doesn't let us race fast, the volume is just going overseas. I can collate my algorithm at any server in the world I choose. So, if you want the United States to be the world's leader in trading and where the world capital comes to trade, you have to create fast and safe tracks for people to race."

The Big Question: Can We Optimize for Something Other than Profit?

The big question becomes what do we optimize for? As Paul, our economist, said, "it gives economists nothing but great consternation to consider optimizing for anything other than profit." And yet it seems we can. Can we adjust? Like Michael Waltrip pointed out, if they take away your ability to adjust your spoiler, then you adjust the car body. Can we be that creative?

What do we need to change?

I went back and talked with Alan Wexelblat, our designer of interfaces for HFT software, and asked, "Can we optimize for something other than profit?"

"Oh, yeah, you can easily optimize for something other than profit," he answered quickly.

"My economist friend Paul thinks I'm crazy for asking the question," I said. "But if you could optimize for something other than profit, what would that be?"

"I can imagine how you could optimize for things like fairness or even quality," Alan continued. "You would just change the signal that you are watching. You would have the algo go out and look for other kinds of information and other kinds of stock."

This goes back to our chocolate cake algo. In the world view of the chocolate cake algo, strawberries do not exist. So we need to expand the recipe.

"How so?" I prodded.

"Well, right now, algos look for liquidity in a stock. That means that the algos look for stocks that are traded a lot," Alan explained. "A stock that is traded a lot could be up or down; doesn't matter. A stock that is traded a lot has more information about it than a stock that people buy and just hold onto. That means that a stock that is traded a lot becomes a stock that is traded a lot. A stock that isn't traded a lot doesn't exist to the algo."

Translated: A stock that isn't traded a lot is a strawberry.

"So what you would do is rewrite the algo to look for something other than liquidity," Alan continued. "You could base that on a lot of things. That could be quality of the company, predictability of the stock. You could reward an algo if it picked a stock that was predictable. You could also spread the activity around." Alan talked faster as he got more excited. "Then you would start looking for small companies and stocks that are new to the market. This kind of thinking is one of the reasons why we have fewer IPOs these days. Who wants to list themselves on a stock market where all the algos are only trading stocks that are already trading? You won't raise any money. There's one way to look at it that says to the algos, you don't exist."

Translated: A new stock that doesn't have a trading history is a strawberry.

"But I don't want it to seem that algos are the only reason that IPOs have dried up," Alan went on to explain. "There are other problems as well and they all feed into each other."

"But you're saying that it's possible to optimize the algorithms to value something other than profit?" I asked.

"Oh, sure, but no one values anything else but profit." Alan chuckled. "But sure. The algos do what we tell them to do. You just have to know what you're optimizing for."

So then I went back to our economist Paul and told him what I'd learned.

"Really," Paul said. "That is interesting. I guess it makes sense, though."

"So how do we define something like fairness or quality so that we can engineer that into the system?" I asked.

"Well the first way would be to allow the social norms

of society moderate profit-maximizing behavior," he answered. "This does happen. Social opinions can change the definition of what is profitable. Fundamentally, this happens whe the profit cureve is reshaped."

"What does that mean?"

"Ok, I have a really harsh example but it's a good one," Paul began. "Once, sadly, shippers profited by carrying slaves from Africa to the Americas. Social revulsion towards slavery may have tempered some of that trade but it took the ban on the slave trade first by the British and ultimately by the U.S. to change the profit curve drastically and leave only outlaws engaged in the trade.

"More prosaic offenses to the environment and the human condition still remain. Social condemnation followed by taxation, regulation, or outlawing of undesirable behavior could change the profit curves for these practices. We have a long way to go to confront the socially unacceptable consequences of some profit-seeking behavior.

"Nevertheless, I strongly suspect that profit-maximization is so robust and so natural to our behavior that we should seek attitudinal and legal changes to alter the profit-maximizing points rather than trying to change human nature and advocating non-sustainable social pursuits by private citizens and firms. It's going to be really hard to optimize for something like fairness," Paul chuckled at me. "Who gets to decide what's fair and what has quality? No one wants to fit into a social order that is maximized for the worst-off person." (Paul is infinitely quotable!)

"But there has to be some place we can start," I pushed.

"You have to remember that even if you design the whole system around fairness and quality," Paul explained, "you are still going to have bad behavior."

"Yes, there will always be crashes and speculation," I agreed.

"So you also have to ask yourself if you really want to live in a system where you have people manipulating fairness and quality to get ahead, because history tells us they will. I would guess that the dark side of that is people abusing power more than profit. At least in the system we have now, we know those devils really well. We understand the perils of profit; we just have to continue to take action. You see"—Paul got a little contemplative—"this never ends. That's the thing about economics and markets and all the things we've been discussing. It never ends. We're never really done trying to make it better."

Futurehunting for Alternative Visions of Futures

There is nothing wrong with profit. In economic terms, it is simply the return of goods or resources to an owner in a productive pursuit of labor. There is something wrong with greed, which is simply the pursuit of excess profit above all other costs. But as Paul pointed out, the problem in that equation is not the profit; it's the excessive part. Even if we did optimize for fairness, then we would have some instances of excessive fairness. Who gets to decide what kind of fairness, and fair to whom? Who profits from the fairness, and who might lose? There will always be bad behavior in the markets, as Sobel's history showed us, and we're always going to have crashes. *It never ends. We're never really done trying to make it better.*

I wanted to see if I could find some real-world examples of people optimizing for something other than profit. But now saying that seems a bit wrong. Profit isn't the real problem; people's bad behavior and excessive use of anything is the real problem. So I wanted to find examples of people optimizing for something new. Companies and individuals who might have ideas counter to the current system. It was another kind of futurehunting. I was looking for examples of alternative futures. These could be futures that might not happen but ones that people were trying hard to make real today.

Richard L. Sandor, Elephant Hunter—No not That Kind

One of the first people who spring to mind when you're looking for alternative models for thinking about the future is Richard Sandor. He started working and experimenting with alternative approaches more than 40 years ago.

I called Richard in his office in Chicago. His learned, relaxed manner brings to mind that college professor whom everyone wanted to have. Richard worked in electronic trading in the 1960s and designed the first system for digital trading. In 2007, he was named the "father of carbon trading" by *Time* magazine for founding the Chicago Climate Exchange (CCX).

"I really wasn't sure if we were going to make any money," Richard explained about starting CCX. "But I did think the issue was important. As it became more popular we saw that powerful companies thought it was the right thing to do. Ford Motor Company joined because they wanted to create a green auto company. The power companies that signed up just thought it was the right thing to do. In the end we had 110 emitters that pledged to reduce their CO_2 emissions by six percent with no law to obligate them to, no government intervention." Although membership was voluntary, members had to comply with the rules and regulations of the exchange and be subject to a third-part verification of their emissions and projects.

At its peak, the CCX's membership represented 17 percent of the companies in the Dow Jones Industrial Average, 20 percent of the largest CO_2-emitting electrical utilities in the United States, and 11 percent of Fortune 100 companies. In 2010 Richard and his associates sold the CCX to the IntercontinentalExchange (ICE) for $600 million.

"So it was a very profitable venture," Richard told me with a chuckle.

At the time of the sale, ICE's founder, Jeffrey Sprecher,

said that Sandor's idea paved the way for Europe's carbon cap-and-trade program. There, the exchange developed into the major platform for trading European Union carbon emissions allowances and certified emission reduction credits generated under the United Nations Clean Development Mechanism.

"Richard, you've shown that people can optimize for something other than profit," I said. "Companies can optimize for profit plus something else, or they could even pursue an alternative approach just because they think it's the right thing to do. So what should people be optimizing for?"

"I like to hunt for elephants," Richard said after a long pause. "I take on tasks that are likely to fail. But if they succeed, then the results will be transformational. It's important that you do something big and important that you believe in." Then after another pause he said, "Bring efficiencies to conserve capital and sustain the well-being of the planet."

Money from People to People

Our banks are broken. The Great Recession of 2008 is still reverberating through the global economy. Five years after the collapse of our banking system, many believe our entire financial system is still in shambles. In the September 23, 2013 issue of *Time* magazine, assistant managing editor Rana Foroohar wrote a scathing and somber appraisal of banking's current state in "The

Myth of Financial Reform."

In the article, she lays out five things we could do to right the current situation. Fix the Too-Big-to-Fail Problem, Limit Leverage, Expose Weapons of Mass Financial Destruction, Bring Shadow Banking into the Light, and Reboot the Culture of Finance. All five areas were both horrific and fascinating to read about, but number five rang true with symptoms I'd been hearing from people in my research.

She wrote, "Banking was created to serve the real economy, not the other way around. But the U.S. economy has gone so far down the path of financialization, becoming so deeply embedded in and beholden to Wall Street, it's hard to remember that the original business of banks was very simple: lending to real people and businesses. The biggest banks make up a larger share of the GDP [Gross Domestic Product] than before the crisis. Yet access to credit for individuals and small businesses that create the majority of new jobs remains tight, and economic growth remains below its long-term trend level." She points out "finance has grown to be a larger percentage of the economy over the past 30 years, new business creation has actually stagnated."

Rana's point is that the business of banks has shifted from lending money to people to making money from money. For most regular folks and new businesses, it's still hard to get money. There is a small group of people who are looking to change this by coming up with an alternative model for banking itself.

Known to some as peer-to-peer lending or consumer lending, it involves people lending money to other people and businesses without a bank. It's unregulated and typically takes place online. I talked with two people with very different backgrounds who are developing companies and imagining a very different future for banking.

Jonathan Ende comes from the banking world. During his career, he's worked at very traditional financial institutions like Lehman Brothers and Bear Stearns. Jonathan left Bear Stearns in 2000 and Lehman in 2005 before they both collapsed in 2008, but the flaws in the banking system drove him to imagine a different future.

He's now founder and CEO of BorrowersFirst™, a newly launched financial tech platform. The idea behind the company is both easy to understand and complex in its implications. BorrowersFirst uses technology to connect borrowers directly with lenders securely and efficiently. The mission is to put borrowers first by giving them direct access to money with better rates and service. The company is launching its credit offerings with personal fixed-rate loans.

"High-interest credit card debt can enslave people. Our goal is to drive down the burden with fixed-rate personal loans that are easy to access, understand and pay back," Jonathan explained. "We're treating consumer credit as a true asset class, making investors compete for the paper so that borrowers benefit. We call it ConnectedCredit™. Consumers are accustomed to shopping online for better choice, price, and service. We want to bring the same efficiency to online borrowing, delivering fast access to affordable credit."

Peter Renton has a very different background. "I come from the label business," he told me, laughing. He had a big Australian laugh. "It was a family business. It did pretty well, and after we sold it, I really wanted to do something different. I think how money is lent and borrowed in 10 years' time will completely change. Online consumer lending will be the norm."

Peter is CEO of Lend Academy, a company like Jonathan's that invests money in people and small businesses often overlooked by banks. The sums can be quite small, so small that a bank would never consider going through the trouble of making the loan.

"Those little sums can really turn people's lives around," Peter told me. "I really think we're giving people access to the American Dream."

"I've talked to a number of different people who think that more effective consumer lending can help turn around the culture of banking," I said. "As a lender, are you optimizing for something other than profit?"

"To optimize for anything other than profit in a free market is difficult," Peter answered. "I think you can optimize for profit *and* something else. What we're doing isn't social entrepreneurship. We're optimizing for profit while directly helping people."

Investing in Personal Reputation

Asheesh Advani has entrepreneurship in his blood.

"I teach MBA students foresight," I told him on a call. "Most of them want to be entrepreneurs, and they always ask my advice as a futurist for what they should do."

"Ok," Asheesh added tentatively.

"I tell them not to do it," I said.

"Really?" Asheesh laughed.

"Yeah," I went on. "I tell them not to do it. Being an entrepreneur is hard, and you're going to fail a lot. I also tell them if they want to make a lot of money, they should just be a dentist. It's more stable, and it will make their parents proud."

Asheesh continued to chuckle.

"Then I tell them they should just leave the class right now and go enroll in dental school or become a registered nurse and help people's lives. Then I pause, and when none of them leave, I tell them good, because if you are an entrepreneur, you can't help it. You'll always be an entrepreneur, even if you are a dentist. It's in the blood."

"I couldn't agree more," Asheesh added.

Asheesh is the CEO of Covestor, an online marketplace that gives people an alternative way of finding and investing in financial portfolio managers. Essentially their company gives people a way to put money into the personal investments of fund managers and some experienced individual investors, who are usually retired from finance but still stay in the game.

"We have 150 portfolio managers," Asheesh explained. "They're not motivated by profit alone. They are trying to make money on their investments, but they are also trying to look good with the investments they make. There's a part of it that's about reputations, fame, and pride. They are motivated to share when they are happy and proud."

"You enable people to make the same investments as your portfolio managers are making with their personal money," I said.

"Yes," Asheesh answered. "It's completely transparent. You do with your money what they are personally doing with their own money. The fund managers even use stories to give people very real accounts about their investing. They explain what they are investing in and why."

"So it's not only a different way to invest your money, it's a different way to pick how that money is invested? People are really investing in the fund manager. They're investing in a person," I added.

"Yes, they are all looking to make money," Asheesh answered. "But how they are looking to make money is not just a profit graph. People are putting their money into the hands of real people, who are transparent about where that money is going and why."

Connecting Humans by Design

Josh Mait has a background in nontraditional qualitative ethnographic work for marketing firms.

"There is a science to relationships," he told me. "I feel like I've learned so much really quickly. Working for a startup is like living in dog years," Josh said, and he laughed. "Everything changes so quickly and moves so fast."

Josh is the chief marketing officer of RelSci—Relationship Science. The company's website explains itself this way:

"The Relationship Science (RelSci) platform contains robust profiles of over two million important decision-makers and the one million organizations they work with across the public, private, finance, and nonprofit sectors. Access to RelSci provides individuals and organizations with the tools to map and build relationships with new clients, potential investors, strategic partners, and other important professionals."

The company cultivates and manages a network of about 2.5 million people and looks to make meaningful connections to people. They don't keep contact information, and they're not a relationship software company.

"A lot of what we do is really the care and feeding of data," Josh explained.

"It sounds like the core of the company is about people," I said. "It's like the foundation of who you are and how you make money is real and meaningful connections to people who want to get things done. Is that what you optimize for?"

"We're optimizing for quality relationships," Josh

answered. "We all know that so much of business is all about who you really know. We facilitate human-to-human communication with openness but at the same time with security and privacy."

The connections that Josh and RelSci make between people are not optimized for profit. Their goal is to connect people; therefore, the qualities and signals that they look for on their platform are fundamentally different. They take time to understand the people in their system and take the time and energy to connect them with people who will have meaningful interactions. Part of the underlying DNA of RelSci is trust. Just like a human-to-human relationship, connecting to people is about establishing trust and allowing it to grow. By definition of the company's goal, RelSci must focus on something other than profit and greed to optimize its business and platform. RelSci succeeds when people succeed—that's both the people in their system and their customers.

A Raging Capitalist Who Wants to Make Money by Being Nice to People

I was on my way to meet Crystal Beasley to talk about a radical idea she had about the future of greed, and I was late. There was traffic. There was parking. My schedule had blown up. I hate being late.

When I got to Blue Hour, I found Crystal sitting at the end of the bar. If you've ever been to Portland, Oregon, and someone wanted to impress you by taking you out to dinner, they probably took you to Blue Hour. It's a staple of Portland's foodie culture, and its soaring ceilings and relaxed modern décor make it fancy without being too fancy.

Crystal is quick and bright and has a thick, thick southern accent that makes me homesick for the Blue Ridge Mountains where I grew up. We started out our chat by seeing which one of us was more white trash. We both came from humble starts, and we declared it a draw.

"So what's your idea?" I got down to business. "I hear you've got a radical notion, but that's all I know."

Crystal smiled and shrugged. "I think we can make more money by being nice to people and not trying to drive them to suicide."

"That sounds like a good idea," I replied.

"No, I mean the whole start-up culture," she explained. "The shotgun approach the venture capitalists take to investing just doesn't work. They make ten bets and hope one will be a raging success, like Facebook or Twitter. They are optimizing for profits, but they are leaving out the humanity."

"So you think there's a different way we could approach investing in startup companies?" I asked.

"Yeah. You can use BP [British Petroleum] as an example," she answered. "As a company they made a decision. They said they wouldn't drill any dry wells, not because they wanted to spare Mother Earth, but because they wanted to maximize their efficiency. To do this they had to become experts in geology. For decades they thought it was acceptable to drill dry wells, but saying that this wasn't acceptable meant that they had to remove all the dark corners where bullshit analysis could hide. They flipped upside down an industry's assumptions about standard operating procedure. Venture capitalists can follow the same path, not because it saves people's lives [literally], but because it's ultimately more profitable."

"The algorithm way of thinking was key for BP," she explained. "They thought they were optimizing for profits but a small tweak to the algorithm actually gave more profit. They were already the world's best experts with the highest hit rate in new wells. Their CEO looked at their analysis and saw that if they rated a well 20 to 70 percent likely of hitting, their predictions were close. But when they rated the well with a 75 percent chance of success, the wells hit nearly all the time. But on the other side when the wells were given a 10 percent rating the chances fell to something like a 1 percent chance."

"Wow."

"I know," she smiled. "Now, BP aren't fools, so why were they drilling any of the below 70 percent wells? The reason was an algorithm that said you take the likelihood and multiply by expected value of the well if it did hit. So, they ended up drilling some unlikely ones that would be big if they did exist. Thing was, they almost never did.

"Their algorithm needed a human analysis step to see if the assessment humans made, in this case, the likelihood of strike, was actually accurate. The algo is only as good as the numbers that are in the spreadsheet. One way or another, those numbers are a human's best attempt to quantify a messy world. You have to complete the feedback loop and see to what degree those humans are doing a good job. Does the recipe, in fact, make a delicious chocolate cake?"

I laughed and nearly spilled my drink. I had explained to Crystal how I explained algorithms to non-engineers. A few weeks later Crystal sent me the quote that inspired her from the from Chip Heath's 2005 book Switch. Heath interviewed executives from BP; Pete Callagher, Jim Farnsworth, and Ian Vann. "The odds-playing gave everyone a false sense of comfort. Hey, if we drill some dry holes, one of the other holes will hit and make up for it. Explorers were like venture capitalists, hoping for and eBay or Google to bail them out of an otherwise lousy portfolio."

"So you're a raging capitalist who wants to make money by being nice to people?" I smiled.

"Yes." She slapped her hand on the bar and laughed. "That's exactly it! You don't have to chew through lots of small companies and their passionate people so that just a few make you money. If you become an expert and actually help those companies, if you change the model, you'll make more money."

Change in the Back Pages

Since starting work on this piece, I've become a bit of a nerd for the back pages of *Bloomberg Markets* magazine. Each month at the back of the magazine is a section called "Strategies." In that section, finance wonks talk about optimizing your data feeds. They talk about everything from "monitoring derivatives" to "tracking variance swaps." It's so specific that they tell you what keystrokes to type to adjust your feeds.

I think I became so fascinated by these complex "how to" articles because they are written by people who are using big data to make specific investment decisions. Each article gives you insight into another way of looking at data and using those data. There's nothing academic about it. The advice is bland, practical, and fascinating.

The July 2013 issued surprised me when I turned to the "Strategies" section and saw the headline "Tracking Company Sustainability." What?

"Weak performance on environmental, social and corporate governance (ESG) criteria may be a warning signal of more-fundamental risks at a company," wrote Gregory Elders, an environmental, social, and governance analyst at Bloomberg in London.

Bloomberg had created an ESG Risk Scorecard to help investors make decisions about investment risk and ranked companies against each other. It seems, like Crystal said, you might be able to make money by being nice to people.

Or conversely, when you are not being nice to people, it might mean that there's really something wrong with your company.

Gregory explained what the scorecard measures: "[It] displays environmental data on energy and water use, greenhouse gas emissions and waste; employee accident and fatality figures; and corporate governance measures such as the independence and composition of the board of directors."

In May of 2013, Bloomberg used the ESG Scorecard to rank "The World's Greenest Banks." Christopher Martin, who covers renewable energy at Bloomberg News in New York, explained how they crunched the numbers to come up with the ranking. *"Bloomberg Markets* looked at [the banks'] efforts to reduce their own waste and carbon footprints and at their investments in clean energy. Bloomberg New Energy Finance and Bloomberg's ESG Data group, which collects information on environmental, social and governance issues, gathered material from annual and corporate social responsibility reports, websites and other public documents. The teams conducted independent research and used surveys and telephone interviews to secure additional data and verify the accuracy of their findings."

All of this exhaustive work led to a tangible ranking for banks based upon their practices. Like the ESG Scorecard asserts, it seemed that optimizing for sustainability, social responsibility, and diversity could be an indicator that your company is healthy. Optimizing for something other than just profit might actually make you more profitable.

Sometimes It's Good to Be Irrational

So what did we learn from all of this futurehunting? Well, it's complicated. Unlike algo trading, when it comes to business, it's almost always about more than just profit. The deeper I looked into people's motives, their companies and why investors made investment decisions, it seemed less about profit and more about what the actual investor was looking for. I began to see that with companies, investors and people, it's actually about profit plus something else. There is room for more than just profit. We have gotten to the point that we can optimize for profit along with something else. People called it profit *plus*. But what is the plus? How do we decide what we are optimizing for? What's the *plus*?

The subtle details of the financial world are that it's really not about profit. People will tell you it is, but it isn't. We live in a world where our financial markets are so complex that *any* investor has a dizzying array of choices. Most will tell you that these are logical decisions, but this too isn't true.

People love to imagine that we are logical beings. We tell ourselves that we are making all of our decisions, especially our financial decisions, based on data. We also tell ourselves that we are ruthlessly optimizing for profit, but the truth is that we humans are incredibly irrational. We don't make decisions based on data. We are emotional; we are value driven. We use data to justify our value-driven decisions.

"You have to understand that this isn't a bad thing," Paul, our economist, said as we discussed this paradox. "I really think that this is one of the reasons why people are so successful. The dirty little secret is that being irrational and value driven actually works for making money. It gives us profit and success."

Optimizing for profit could actually mean following your values. The secret could be that profit and values are tightly intertwined. If we are optimizing for our values then, I guess the questions are now, what are your values? Have you thought about it? What do you value?

Part Five

THE NATURE OF EVIL AND OUR BETTER ANGELS

The project was almost done, and I needed to think. I knew the implications of this work went far beyond greed and the future of our financial systems. One of the foundational ideas behind this series is that humans and machines are inextricably linked. In a future where our lives are intensely intertwined with our machines and technology, it seems we need to think differently about that relationship.

When I need to think, I go to bookstores. Powell's Books is my hometown bookstore and one of the best on the planet. I walked the stacks, thinking about humanity's relationship with our technology. In the science section, I found a book called *The Children of Frankenstein: A Primer on Modern Technology and Human Values*, written by Herbet J. Muller, an American historian, academic, and government official. One of the great things about Powell's is that they mix new and used books. Muller's book was his last and was published in 1970, before the transformation of our technological world by computers and the Internet. But many of the ideas and issues that Muller struggles with apply to today. My edition of the book has a striking cover. On a green background, yellow lines outline human figures with digital numbers and figures over their faces. It's both dated and haunting.

Muller writes, "My experience has been that a deeper understanding of a technical society gives better reasons for fear of life in it."

The Nature of Evil

George Orwell, the journalist and author of *1984*, wrote that the dream of a just society "seems to haunt the human imagination ineradicably and in all ages, whether it is called the Kingdom of Heaven or the classless society or whether it is thought of as a Golden Age which once existed in the past and from which we have degenerated."

We have spent most of this book dreaming of and imagining a just society. The implication of what could come after greed is that it could be something better. How do we get beyond our own bad behavior? Profit in and of itself is not bad. It is the excessive pursuit of profit that is greed. So if we are asking what comes after greed, then we are really asking how we guard against our own shortcomings.

Many of the people I talked to showed us that there has always been bad behavior. The history of financial markets is a history of panics and crashes. It does seem that it all is like a NASCAR race and we are all drivers like Michael Waltrip who just don't think about the crashes. We are more worried about letting our team down.

It makes us question our own human nature. If we imbue our machines with our own humanity, then are we imbuing it with our flaws as well? Can we imbue our technology with the dark side of humanity? Algo trading is a pretty clear instantiation of greed when we let the algorithms run free. How do we guard against that? Could we imbue our machines with evil?

Michael Foley is an Irish novelist and poet living in London. His first nonfiction book was called *The Age of Absurdity: Why Modern Life Makes It Hard to Be Happy* (2010). In the book, Foley explores the thorny problem of happiness in our modern world. In his search to understand happiness, Foley does an amazing job of describing the nature of evil.

"The alternative to thinking is not emotion but thoughtlessness. Failing to think may sound like a harmless form of addiction—but Hannah Arendt was vouchsafed a profound insight while attending the trial of the Nazi Adolf Eichmann in Jerusalem. Attempting to understand his motivation, she considered—but was forced to reject—the traditional idea of evil as a positive, demonic force i.e. original sin or Manichean explanation. Then came the insight: Eichmann's most notable characteristic was not ideological conviction, nor was it evil motivation but *thoughtlessness*. In the Israeli court he functioned, as he had done in Germany, by sticking to clichéd, conventional language that protects against reality and renders thinking unnecessary. Arendt's conclusion (written in 2001): 'Could the activity of thinking as such, the habit of examining whatever comes to pass or to attract attention, regardless of results and specific content, could this activity be among the conditions that make men abstain from evil-doing or even actually "condition" them against it.'"

Foley sums it up by writing, "So thinking may make the difference between good and evil."

The technology doesn't get to decide what it gets to do. Humans get to decide. The algos that crashed the stock market were taught to do it by the traders who programmed them; the programmers defined the world.

Ultimately this isn't about data or algorithms or computers. It's about people. This is a social, cultural, and uniquely human discussion. We have to ask ourselves what we value. What are we optimizing for? Fairness? Quality? Safety? Social responsibility? Then we need to define and understand the dark side of what we are optimizing for, because there will be a dark side. What is the dark side of quality? What are the demons of social responsibility? What is the underbelly of fairness?

But most importantly, we need to talk about it. We

need to tell each other what we value and then argue about it, because that's how we make change. As a futurist, I tell people that we have to remember that the future involves everyone. The future includes people you don't agree with. And the thing that's hard for most people to accept is that the future involves people you don't even like.

But we still need to do something. If the future is built every day by the actions of people, then the real work of the future is talking about it and then acting. We can't sit back and worry about the machines becoming too intelligent and taking over. We must remain in control of our tools. The way we remain in control is by *thinking* about it.

From all the people I talked to, I've seen that the very act of asking *what are you optimizing for?* is what's important. The act of thinking and discussing what you value is the key to warding off the bad behavior that seems inevitable. Understanding that we imbue our technology and machines with our humanity means we need to identify and *think* about what we are building, why we are building it, and what we want our tools to accomplish.

People often come up to me and are worried that if we make the machines too smart, then we humans will become stupid. This worries me. Intelligence isn't finite. If we give intelligence to algorithms and machines, it doesn't mean we take it away from ourselves. I find this notion frightening because it undervalues how awesome we can be as human beings. We are giving away our power over the future by simply doing nothing.

Doing nothing is the nature of evil. Not thinking is dangerous. We need to have an opinion, to take a position, and understand that we are building our futures with the machines and technology we are developing.

At the end of Muller's *The Children of Frankenstein*, he captures what we might need to do. "We cannot afford to lose all our dreams of a just society, lest the injustice that has always been with us has a still easier time. Or if we are going to 'think about the unthinkable' we may need to dream simply to preserve our sanity. The real challenge remains that we do possess the technical means of doing almost anything we have a mind to, short of making angels of men. Today wide visions of ideal ends are more necessary than before."

Our Better Angels

If all this technology is simply a tool and we humans fill our tools with our values, hopes, and dreams of the future, then we need to take control of the art. Be present and aware of what we are doing. We need to ask each other what we value. What are we optimizing for? And then start building.

We can design better algorithms and better technology. We can design our technology to know us and value us. But to do that, we need to know ourselves and value ourselves and others. If we do this, then we have designed technology that allows us to be more human. Technology doesn't take away from our humanity; it amplifies it.

And I challenge you that we can go one step further. If we know what we are optimizing for and we are using all this intelligence to make the lives of people better, then we can not only design technology that allows us to be more human, we can also design technology that makes us better humans. Human beings will always have demons. There will always be crashes and panics, and our work is never really done. While I was writing this piece, the NASDAQ shut down twice because of "technical issues." Trading stopped, sending an eerie silence across the financial sector. It seems that there are still many problems inside the black box of finance, and algo trading is just the tip of the iceberg.

But if we can change how we think about our relationship with technology, then it just might be possible to live with our demons but build technology to be our better angels. They can be a reflection of our best selves, and that's something pretty awesome to be optimizing for.

Masahiro Mori is a legendary roboticist and thinker. In 1970s Japan, Mori-san developed the now-famous idea of the Uncanny Valley, which explored how humans and robots interact with each other. Mori-san was a pioneer in his understanding of how people and their machines could live together.

In his 1974 book *The Buddha in the Robot*, Mori-san wrote, "Machines, let us observe, are not intrinsically bad. The problem lies with people, who rarely make an effort to understand the machinery they use. If we know machines and give them a chance to do what they do well, they can be valuable comrades and helpers."

But Mori-san pushed us to think further. In *The Buddha in the Robot*, Mori-san also wrote, "Human beings have self or ego, but machines have none at all. Does this lack cause machines to do crazy, irresponsible things? Not at all. It is people with their egos, who are constantly being led by selfish desires to commit unspeakable deeds. The root of man's lack of freedom (insofar as he actually lacks it) is his egocentrism. In this sense, the ego-less machine leads a less hampered existence." Freed from selfishness and ego, robots and machines actually have the ability to rise above petty human troubles and attain a high level of existence. In this way, Mori-san said that robots are closer to the Buddha-nature.

What if our technology could provide an example for us? If a machine is simply a tool to echo our humanity, what if the humanity it shows back to us is even more pure, even more enlightened than the humans who crafted it? What can we learn from our technology? What can it teach us?

PART SIX

Epilogue: Don't Call Your Mother!

As I was finishing this piece, I heard a great and prag-matic real-world example of how we could work as I have described with our technology today.

I was in the labs of Intel talking with Dr. Genevieve Bell—you remember her from earlier—and we were talk-ing about how technology can lead us into better behavior.

"We have all these sensors and intelligence and smart gadgets…well, imagine your smartphone or smart home or smart whatever knew you. It knew how you felt. It followed what you did and *cared* about it," she explained. "Now imagine if your phone knew that you called your mother every Thursday at 4:30 pm before heading home from work."

"That makes sense," I added.

"Now most people would say that if your phone knew that you called your mother at 4:30 every Thursday it would pull up that application on your phone and even make sure your phone and your mom's phone were talking to each other and that your mother was near the phone."

"I'm following," I said. "It's all pretty simple predictive computing. Your devices are smart enough to know what you do and when you do it, so why shouldn't they get themselves ready and make your life easier?"

"Right," she said, and smiled, holding up a finger. "Now imagine that your devices and data also knew that at 4:45 pm each day when you got off the phone with your mother you were always depressed and anxious and upset."

I snorted out loud.

"Right!" She held up her hands. "Imagine your data and devices knew that usually means that every Thursday you then went online and bought too many shoes when you got home to make yourself feel better."

"That's understandable," I added.

"With all that in mind, why wouldn't your phone stop you from making the call?" she asked. "Imagine when you picked up the phone to call your mother at 4:30 pm your phone said, 'Hey Brian, maybe you shouldn't call you mom right now. It usually upsets you and gets her upset as well. How about giving her a call on Saturday afternoon—that usually goes better for the both of you.'"

Now, that's an application we could all get behind!

The idea here is that our data and computational intelligence can understand us in very simple ways and make helpful suggestions to give us better relationships with people. This is just a short-term pragmatic example, but we can imagine how our technologies, the code, and all the machines we are building can be our better angels. They can give us just a little nudge in the right direction. And if we are present and understand what we are optimizing for, then they could improve our relationships, improve our health, and truly exemplify our best selves.

Brian David Johnson

The future is Brian David Johnson's business. As a futurist he develops an actionable 10-15 year vision for the future of technology and what it will feel like to live in the future. His work is called "futurecasting"—using ethnographic field studies, technology research, trend data, and even science fiction to provide a pragmatic vision of consumers and computing. Johnson works with governments, militaries, trade organizations and corporations. He is currently the resident futurist for the Intel Corporation. He speaks and writes extensively about future technologies in articles (The Wall Street Journal, Slate, IEEE Computer, Successful Farming) and both science fiction and fact books (Vintage Tomorrows, Science Fiction Prototyping, Screen Future and Fake Plastic Love). Johnson lectures around the world and teaches as a professor at The University of Washington and The California College of the Arts MBA program. He appears regularly on Bloomberg TV, PBS, FOX News, and the Discovery Channel and has been featured in Scientific American, The Technology Review, Forbes, INC, and Popular Science. He has directed two feature films and is an illustrator and commissioned painter.

9804844R20058

Made in the USA
San Bernardino, CA
28 March 2014